# simple

Produced by **ACP**books

Printed by Bookbuilders, China.
Published by ACP Publishing Pty Limited, 54 Park Street, Sydney, NSW 2001 (GPO Box 4088, Sydney, NSW 1028),
phone (02) 9282 8618, fax (02) 9267 9438, acpbooks@acp.com.au  www.acpbooks.com.au
AUSTRALIA: Distributed by Network Services, GPO Box 4088, Sydney, NSW 1028, phone (02) 9282 8777, fax (02) 9264 3278.
UNITED KINGDOM: Distributed by Australian Consolidated Press (UK), Moulton Park Business Centre, Red House Road,
Moulton Park, Northampton, NN3 6AQ, phone (01604) 497 531, fax (01604) 497 533, acpukltd@aol.com
CANADA: Distributed by Whitecap Books Ltd, 351 Lynn Avenue, North Vancouver, BC, V7J 2C4,
phone (604) 980 9852, fax (604) 980 8197, customerservice@whitecap.ca  www.whitecap.ca
NEW ZEALAND: Distributed by Netlink Distribution Company, ACP Media Centre, Cnr Fanshawe and Beaumont Streets,
Westhaven, Auckland (PO Box 47906, Ponsonby, Auckland, NZ), phone (9) 366 9966, ask@ndcnz.co.nz

Gourmet simple.
Includes index.
ISBN 1 86396 286 7.
1. Cookery. 2. Quick and easy cookery. I. Australian Gourmet Traveller.
641.6374
© ACP Publishing Pty Limited 2003
ABN 18 053 273 546
Front cover: Mixed pea and prawn linguine, page 58.

**AUSTRALIAN GOURMET TRAVELLER**
**Editor-in-chief** Judy Sarris
**Food editor** Leanne Kitchen
**Deputy food editor** Sophia Young
**Assistant food editor** Christine Osmond

**ACP BOOKS**
**Editorial director** Susan Tomnay
**Creative director** Hieu Chi Nguyen
**Senior editor** Lynda Wilton
**Publishing manager (sales)** Jennifer McDonald
**Publishing manager (rights & new projects)** Jane Hazell
**Brand manager** Donna Giannotis
**Production manager** Carol Currie
**Business manager** Sally Lees
**Studio manager** Caryl Wiggins
**Pre-press** Harry Palmer
**Editorial coordinator** Holly van Oyen
**Editorial assistant** Lana Meldrum

**Photographer** John Paul Urizar
**Stylist** Kristen Anderson
**Recipes by**
Vanessa Broadfoot, Bronwen Clark, Jane Hann,
Kathleen Gandy, Leanne Kitchen, Lynne Mullins,
Louise Pickford, Jody Vassallo, Sophia Young
**Food preparation by**
Amanda Biffin, Christine Sheppard, Rodney Dunn

**Chief executive officer** John Alexander
**Group publisher** Jill Baker
**Publisher** Sue Wannan

THANKS TO THESE STOCKISTS AND SUPPLIERS
Accoutrement phone (02) 9969 1031 or (02) 9418 2992
The Bay Tree phone (02) 9328 1101
Country Road HomeWear phone 1800 801 911
Demcos Seafoods phone (02) 9700 9000
Design Mode International phone (02) 9998 8200
Empire Homewares phone (02) 9380 8877
G&C Ventura phone (02) 9555 7277
Ici Et La phone (02) 9699 4266
Jarass phone (02) 9436 2929
Malcolm Greenwood phone (02) 9953 8613
Mrs Red & Sons phone (02) 9310 4860
Mud Australia phone (02) 9518 0220
Orrefors Kosta Boda (head office) phone (02) 9913 4200
Orson & Blake phone (02) 9326 1155
Papaya phone (02) 9362 1620
Planet Furniture phone (02) 9698 0680 or 0414 777 267
Shack phone (02) 9884 7332
Simon Johnson Purveyor of Quality Foods phone (02) 9319 6122
Spence & Lyda phone (02) 9212 6747
Vic's Premium Quality Meat phone (02) 9667 3922
Wheel & Barrow phone (02) 9938 4555

# simple

ACPbooks

# contents

# soups

From lush, smooth purées to chunky meals-in-a-pot, soups are always best when flavours are kept simple. Winter calls for soothing, steaming bowlsful, made rich with cheese, cream or pungent herb pastes, while warm-weather soups, sometimes served chilled, are palate-refreshing affairs, awakening appetites jaded by summer's heat.

## Chilled avocado soup with prawns

2 large ripe avocados, halved, seeded and peeled
1 clove of garlic, finely chopped
⅓ cup lime juice
Pinch of cayenne
1.25 litres cold chicken stock
12 cooked king prawns (about 600g),
 shelled, cleaned and finely chopped

Process avocados, garlic, lime juice and cayenne in a food processor until mixture is smooth. Add chicken stock, process until well combined, then season to taste with sea salt and freshly ground black pepper. Divide soup among 6 glasses or bowls, top with chopped prawns and serve.

Soup will keep, in an airtight container in the refrigerator, for 1 day.
**Serves 6**

# Chilled carrot, tomato and sherry soup

2½ tablespoons olive oil

1 onion, chopped

500g carrots, chopped

1 teaspoon ground cumin

1 teaspoon sweet paprika

Pinch of cayenne, optional

1.5kg vine-ripened tomatoes,
    peeled and chopped

2-2½ cups chicken or vegetable stock

260ml dry sherry

Croûtons, to serve

Heat oil in a large saucepan, add onion and carrots and cook, covered, stirring frequently, over medium heat until vegetables are soft. Add cumin, paprika and cayenne, if using, and cook, uncovered, for 2-3 minutes. Stir in tomatoes and 2 cups stock, and simmer for 15 minutes or until tomatoes are very soft.

Pass tomato mixture through a mouli, or process in a food processor until smooth, then push through a sieve for a finer texture. Stir in sherry and a little more stock if soup is too thick, and season to taste. Cool soup to room temperature, then cover and refrigerate for several hours. Serve soup topped with croûtons.

Serves 4-6

# Provençal-style flageolet bean and vegetable soup with pistou

125g (½ cup) dried flageolet beans,
  soaked in cold water overnight, then drained
2 tablespoons olive oil
1 onion, thinly sliced
1 leek, thinly sliced
600g jap pumpkin, peeled,
  seeded and cut into 1cm pieces
1 large carrot, cut into 1cm pieces
2 zucchini, cut into 1cm pieces
100g green beans, cut into 2cm pieces

Pistou
½ cup (firmly packed) basil leaves
3 cloves of garlic
60g (¾ cup) grated parmesan
⅓ cup olive oil

For pistou, process basil and garlic in a food processor until finely chopped, then add cheese and process until combined. With motor running, gradually add olive oil in a thin, steady stream until a paste forms. Season to taste.

Cook flageolet beans in a large saucepan of boiling water for 50-60 minutes or until just tender, then drain.

Meanwhile, heat oil in a large saucepan, add onion and leek and cook over low heat for 10 minutes or until soft, then add pumpkin and carrot and stir over medium heat for 3 minutes. Add 1.5 litres water and simmer for 5 minutes, add flageolet beans, zucchini and 2 teaspoons salt and simmer for 15 minutes, then add green beans and simmer for another 5 minutes or until all vegetables are tender. Season to taste. Remove from heat and stir in three-quarters of the pistou. Serve soup in warm bowls topped with a spoonful of remaining pistou.

**Serves 6**

## Cheese and bread soup

Traditional Italian bread soups such as *pappa al pomodoro* are not soupy at all, as the bread soaks up the liquid. For this recipe, adjust the consistency to your taste.

⅓ cup olive oil
350g day-old Italian-style bread, crust removed and cut into 1cm pieces
3 cloves of garlic, finely chopped
1 dried, small red chilli, crumbled
3 large ripe egg tomatoes, peeled and chopped
6-7 cups hot chicken stock
100g pecorino, finely grated

Heat olive oil in a large saucepan, add bread and cook, tossing occasionally, over low-medium heat for 3-5 minutes or until crisp and golden. Add garlic and chilli and stir for 1-2 minutes or until fragrant. Add tomatoes and stir for 3-5 minutes or until heated through, then add 6 cups hot chicken stock and simmer gently for 20 minutes or until bread is very soft and mixture quite thick.

Adjust the consistency of the soup, if desired, by adding a little more hot chicken stock, then stir in one-quarter of the pecorino and season to taste with sea salt and freshly ground black pepper.

Serve immediately, ladled into warm bowls, sprinkled with remaining pecorino.

Serves 4-6

# Saigon noodle soup

2 litres chicken stock

8 black peppercorns

2cm piece of ginger, thinly sliced

1 clove of garlic, crushed

1 onion, thinly sliced

¼ cup crisp fried shallots, plus extra, to serve

1 tablespoon fish sauce

3 teaspoons light soy sauce

2 chicken breast fillets, trimmed

375g dried rice stick noodles

12 green king prawns, shelled and cleaned,
    leaving tails intact

100g (1¼ cups) beansprouts, tailed

¼ cup mint leaves

2 tablespoons chopped coriander leaves

Sliced green onions, sliced red chillies,
    sprigs of coriander and lime wedges, to serve

Combine chicken stock, peppercorns, ginger, garlic, onion, crisp fried shallots, fish sauce and soy sauce in a large saucepan and bring to the boil, then simmer gently over low-medium heat for 5 minutes. Add chicken and gently simmer for 12-15 minutes or until just cooked through. Remove chicken, cool slightly, then slice and set aside. Strain stock, discarding solids, then return stock to a clean saucepan, season to taste and bring to a simmer.

Meanwhile, cook noodles in boiling water for 6-8 minutes or until just tender, then drain well. Divide noodles among 4 bowls. Add prawns to simmering stock and cook for 2-3 minutes or until just cooked, then, using a slotted spoon, place 3 prawns and a few chicken slices in each bowl. Top with beansprouts, mint and coriander, then ladle over stock. Serve immediately topped with green onions, red chillies, sprigs of coriander and extra crisp fried shallots, with lime wedges to the side.

**Serves 4**

## Roast parsnip and cumin soup

1kg parsnips, peeled and chopped
1 large onion, sliced
2 teaspoons cumin seeds
4 cloves of garlic, unpeeled
200g sebago potatoes, peeled and chopped
¼ cup olive oil
1 litre chicken stock
½ cup pouring cream

Combine parsnips, onion, cumin seeds, garlic and potatoes in a roasting pan, drizzle with olive oil and season to taste, then mix to coat well. Roast, stirring occasionally, at 210C for 25 minutes or until vegetables are lightly browned and tender.

Peel garlic, process with half the vegetable mixture and half the chicken stock in a food processor until smooth, then transfer to a large saucepan. Repeat with remaining vegetable mixture and stock. Bring soup to the boil, add cream and season to taste, then stir over medium heat until warmed through. Serve soup immediately in warmed bowls, sprinkled with freshly ground black pepper.

Serves 8

# salads

The crunch and snap of perfectly fresh produce deserve the simplest of treatments. Leaves, herbs and just-cooked vegetables team brilliantly with meats or seafood, nuts and seeds, unctuous cheese or chewy grains to suit the mood of the season. Crusty, rustic bread, either torn at the table or sliced and toasted, is the only accompaniment needed to create a satisfying lunch, dinner or supper.

## Roasted beetroot and spanish onion salad with almonds

1 bunch beetroot (about 750g), peeled and cut into wedges
2 large spanish onions, peeled and cut into wedges
⅓ cup extra virgin olive oil
1 tablespoon aged red wine vinegar
80g blanched whole almonds, roasted
120g semi-dried tomatoes
100g baby spinach leaves
150g firm goat's cheese, crumbled
Crusty bread, to serve

Place beetroot, spanish onions and 2 tablespoons olive oil in a large roasting pan, season to taste with sea salt and freshly ground black pepper, combine well and roast at 200C for 45 minutes, turning occasionally, or until tender. Transfer roasted vegetables to a large bowl, add remaining olive oil, red wine vinegar, almonds, semi-dried tomatoes and spinach, and combine well. Divide warm salad between 6 plates, scatter with crumbled goat's cheese and serve with crusty bread.
**Serves 6 as an entrée or accompaniment**

# Pearl barley, apple and prosciutto salad

200g (1 cup) pearl barley
2 pink lady apples, cored and thinly sliced
Olive oil
225g (15 slices) prosciutto, halved crosswise
1 tablespoon chopped thyme leaves
½ cup extra virgin olive oil
¼ cup red wine vinegar, or to taste
Washed-rind cheese, to serve

Cook barley in plenty of boiling salted water for
35 minutes or until very tender. Drain and cool.
    Meanwhile, brush apple slices with oil and char-grill,
in batches, over medium-high heat, until soft. In a large
bowl, toss barley, apple, prosciutto, thyme, extra virgin
olive oil and vinegar and season to taste. Serve with
cheese, passed separately.
Serves 6

# Pancetta, pea, lentil and mint salad

225g Puy lentils or other French-style fine green lentils

2 small onions, finely chopped

300g piece of pancetta or speck, chopped

150g baby green beans, trimmed

200g sugarsnap peas, trimmed

350g peas, podded

2½ tablespoons lemon juice

100ml olive oil

¼ cup coarsely chopped mint

Place lentils and onions in a large saucepan, cover with plenty of water and bring to the boil, then simmer over medium heat for 30-35 minutes or until lentils are tender. Drain, then transfer to a large bowl.

Meanwhile, add pancetta to a hot non-stick frying pan and cook, stirring occasionally, over medium heat for 5-8 minutes or until browned.

Add baby green beans to a saucepan of boiling salted water and cook for 2 minutes, then add sugarsnap peas and peas and cook for another 2-3 minutes or until peas and beans are tender, then drain. Add beans, peas and pancetta to lentils with remaining ingredients, season to taste and toss well to combine.

**Serves 4**

# Ocean trout, celeriac and saffron remoulade

800g piece ocean trout,
    pin-boned
700g celeriac (about 1 bulb)
¼ cup chopped flat-leaf parsley
4 cups watercress sprigs
Saffron and garlic mayonnaise
½ teaspoon saffron threads
2 egg yolks
1 tablespoon Dijon mustard
1 clove of garlic, finely chopped
2 tablespoons lemon juice
1 cup olive oil

For saffron and garlic mayonnaise, soak saffron in 2 tablespoons hot water for 30 minutes. Combine saffron mixture, egg yolks, mustard, garlic and lemon juice in a food processor and process until well combined. With motor running, add olive oil a little at a time until mixture begins to thicken, then add remaining oil in a slow, steady stream. Season to taste.

Steam trout, skin-side down, covered, in a steamer over boiling water for 6 minutes or until just cooked – trout should still be pink in middle. Cool trout to room temperature, remove skin, then coarsely flake and season to taste.

Peel celeriac, then cut into julienne, placing in a bowl of acidulated water as you go. Blanch celeriac, in batches, in boiling salted water, for 30 seconds, then refresh in iced water, drain well and pat dry on absorbent paper. Combine trout, celeriac, parsley, watercress and mayonnaise in a large bowl and gently toss to coat in mayonnaise. Serve immediately.

**Serves 6**

# Spinach, sesame and chicken salad

2 chicken breast fillets
2 slices of lemon
6 black peppercorns
500g baby spinach leaves
200g frozen shelled soy beans
1 tablespoon lemon juice

Sesame dressing
35g (¼ cup) sesame seeds
1 tablespoon sugar
¼ cup soy sauce
1 tablespoon mirin
¼ cup dashi

For sesame dressing, dry-roast sesame seeds in a frying pan over medium heat until golden. Transfer to a mortar and pound with a pestle until seeds are coarsely crushed. Add sugar, soy sauce, mirin and dashi and stir to combine.

Place chicken in a deep frying pan, cover with water and bring to a gentle simmer. Add lemon slices and peppercorns and gently poach chicken for 10 minutes or until tender. Drain and cool slightly, then shred.

Steam spinach and soy beans separately in the top of a covered steamer over boiling water until tender. Place vegetables in the centre of each plate, drizzle with lemon juice and top with shredded chicken. Pour dressing over and serve immediately.

**Serves 4 as an entrée**

# Spanish-style warm potato and mussel salad with paprika dressing

160ml dry white wine

1 onion, finely chopped

2kg black mussels, scrubbed and bearded

1kg kipfler potatoes, scrubbed

1 clove of garlic, crushed

1 teaspoon Spanish sweet paprika

100ml olive oil

2 tablespoons white wine vinegar

4 green onions, thinly sliced

½ cup flat-leaf parsley leaves

Combine white wine, onion and mussels in a large saucepan and bring to the boil over medium heat, cover with a tight-fitting lid and steam for 3-5 minutes or until shells open.

Using a slotted spoon, transfer mussels to a bowl, discarding any unopened mussels. Strain cooking liquid into a clean saucepan and simmer over medium heat until reduced to ⅓ cup.

Remove mussels from shells and place in a large bowl.

Cook potatoes in boiling salted water until tender, then drain. When cool enough to handle, slice thickly on the diagonal and add to mussels.

Combine reduced mussel cooking liquid, garlic, paprika, olive oil and vinegar in a small bowl and whisk until well combined, season to taste and pour over warm salad in bowl. Add remaining ingredients and toss gently to combine. Serve immediately.

Serves 4-6 as a light lunch or entrée

# Broccolini with hazelnut dressing and fresh cheese

2 bunches broccolini (500g), 1cm trimmed from ends
⅓ cup olive oil
1 large clove of garlic, very thinly sliced
2 tablespoons black olive tapenade
1 tablespoon balsamic vinegar
45g roasted hazelnuts, peeled and coarsely chopped
Toasted ciabatta or Italian-style bread, to serve
200g fresh cheese, such as ricotta or goat's curd

Steam broccolini over a pan of simmering water for 6-8 minutes or until tender. Drain broccolini, reserving 2 tablespoons of cooking water.

Heat olive oil in a small frying pan, add garlic and cook over low heat until light golden. Add tapenade and balsamic vinegar and whisk until well combined.

Place broccolini, reserved cooking water, tapenade mixture and chopped hazelnuts in a large bowl, season to taste with freshly ground black pepper and toss to combine. Serve toasts spread with fresh cheese and topped with broccolini mixture.

Serves 6

# vegetables

Purées, stir-fries, frittatas, salads: the possibilities for sensational, simple ways with fresh vegetables are without limit. Unrivalled for their versatility, vegetables sit well at any stage of a meal – appetiser, entrée, main course or accompaniment. Let mushrooms on toast star at brunch, sweet potato fritters serve as lunch, or a chunky pumpkin pie with goat's cheese satisfy for dinner.

## Fennel and white bean purée

¼ cup olive oil
1 large bulb of fennel (about 600g), trimmed
    and chopped, plus fennel tops, to serve
2 cloves of garlic, finely chopped
420g can cannellini beans, rinsed and drained
2 tablespoons lemon juice
Sourdough bread, sliced and toasted, to serve

Heat olive oil in a heavy-based saucepan, add fennel and stir to coat with oil. Cover and cook over low heat for 20 minutes, stirring frequently, then add garlic and cook, covered, for another 5 minutes or until fennel is very soft. Process fennel mixture, drained cannellini beans and lemon juice in a food processor until smooth, then season to taste with sea salt and freshly ground black pepper. Serve purée, scattered with fennel tops, with toasted sourdough or with fish or roast meats.
Makes about 2 cups
Serves 6 as an appetiser or as a vegetable accompaniment

# Middle Eastern vegetable salad

600g chat potatoes, halved

Olive oil

2 red capsicum, seeded and
   cut into 1cm strips

1 large eggplant (about 550g), halved
   lengthways and thickly sliced

1 teaspoon ground coriander

1 teaspoon sweet paprika

400g can chickpeas, drained
   and rinsed

120g (¾ cup) kalamata olives

2 tablespoons extra virgin olive oil

1 tablespoon pomegranate molasses

¼ cup coriander leaves

Combine potatoes and 1 tablespoon olive oil in
a roasting pan, then roast at 200C for 30 minutes.
Add capsicum to pan and cook for another
30 minutes or until vegetables are tender and
potatoes are golden. Place eggplant slices in
a large bowl with ¼ cup olive oil, coriander
and paprika and combine well. Char-grill or
barbecue eggplant, turning once, until golden
and tender, then combine with roasted
vegetables and remaining ingredients.
Season to taste and serve warm with grilled
or roasted meat or poultry.

Serves 6

## Pumpkin and goat's cheese pie

700g butternut pumpkin, peeled,
   seeded and cut into 2cm pieces
1 teaspoon cumin seeds
Olive oil
120g firm goat's cheese, crumbled
1 cup flat-leaf parsley leaves
6 sheets filo pastry
Green salad, to serve

Place pumpkin and cumin seeds in a roasting pan, drizzle with 2 tablespoons olive oil, season to taste with sea salt and freshly ground black pepper and toss to combine well. Roast at 200C for 45 minutes, turning once during cooking, or until tender and starting to brown on edges. Cool, then combine with goat's cheese and parsley.

Working with one sheet of filo pastry at a time, lightly brush sheets with olive oil and fold in half lengthwise, then brush top with olive oil. Place sheets, slightly overlapping, to cover base and side of a 22cm springform tin, extending ends over edge of tin. Spoon pumpkin mixture evenly into pastry shell, smoothing top even. Brush overhanging pastry with olive oil and fold over pie in an overlapping pattern. Brush top with olive oil, then bake at 200C for 30 minutes or until pastry is golden and crisp. Stand for 10 minutes, then serve slices with a green salad.

**Serves 4-6 as an entrée or light meal**

# Kecap manis-glazed tofu and asian greens

300g packet firm tofu, cut into 1x2cm slices

¼ cup peanut oil

3 bunches mixed asian greens, such as choy sum,
    bok choy, gai lum or ung choy (water spinach),
    cut into bite-sized pieces

2 cloves of garlic, crushed with a pinch of salt

1 tablespoon ginger, cut into julienne

1-2 teaspoons sambal oelek

2½ tablespoons kecap manis

1 tablespoon mushroom oyster sauce

2 tablespoons vegetable or chicken stock

Steamed rice or noodles, crisp fried shallots and
    sliced red chillies, to serve

Using absorbent paper, carefully pat tofu dry. Heat a wok over high heat, add 2 tablespoons oil, swirling to coat wok, then fry tofu, in batches, for 2-3 minutes or until brown, taking care that it does not break up. Remove and set aside. Heat remaining oil in wok and stir-fry asian greens, in batches, until stems are tender but still firm and leaves are wilted. Remove vegetables from wok and set aside. Add garlic, ginger and sambal oelek and stir-fry for 30 seconds, then add kecap manis, oyster sauce and stock and bring to the boil; simmer for 1 minute or until sauce is reduced. Return vegetables to wok with tofu, then toss gently until coated in sauce. Serve tofu and asian greens on a bed of steamed rice or noodles, topped with crisp fried shallots and sliced red chillies.

**Serves 4**

# Mushrooms on toast

40g butter

200g swiss brown mushrooms, halved

100g shiitake mushrooms, halved

150g shimeji mushrooms, whole

2 cloves of garlic, finely chopped

¼ cup verjuice

200ml (¾ cup) crème fraîche

2 tablespoons marjoram leaves

2 tablespoons chopped chives

Wilted spinach and sourdough toast, to serve

Melt butter in a large non-stick frying pan, add swiss brown and shiitake mushrooms and cook over high heat for 5 minutes or until mushrooms are almost cooked. Add shimeji mushrooms and garlic and cook for another 1 minute, then add verjuice and bring to the boil. Stir in crème fraîche and herbs, season to taste with sea salt and freshly ground black pepper and cook until just warmed through. Serve immediately on a bed of wilted spinach with sourdough toast.

Serves 4 as a breakfast or light meal

## Fontina fondue

500g fontina, coarsely grated
1 cup milk
4 egg yolks
Sweet paprika, cubes of rustic
    bread, steamed kipfler potatoes,
    cornichons and steamed
    broccolini, to serve

Place fontina in a heatproof bowl, pour milk over, cover and refrigerate for 1 hour.

Place fontina mixture over a saucepan of gently simmering water and stir gently (the cheese will look stringy at first) until cheese just melts and mixture is smooth. Add egg yolks, one at a time, whisking after each, until well combined, then stir for another 3-5 minutes or until mixture is smooth and heated through. Do not overheat. Serve immediately, poured into small bowls and sprinkled with paprika, with plates of rustic bread, steamed kipfler potatoes, cornichons and steamed broccolini for dipping.

**Makes about 2 cups**
Serves 4-6

# Sweet potato fritters with avocado purée

Peanut oil

800g orange sweet potato,
   peeled and coarsely grated

6 green onions, chopped

6 kaffir-lime leaves, centre vein removed,
   thinly shredded

½ cup coriander leaves

2 fresh red serrano chillies,
   seeded and finely chopped

75g (½ cup) plain flour

3 eggs, separated

150g (1 cup) sesame seeds

Baby rocket leaves, to serve

Avocado purée

1 large avocado, seeded,
   peeled and coarsely chopped

1 tablespoon lime juice

1 tablespoon sour cream

For avocado purée, process all ingredients in a food processor until smooth, season to taste, then cover and refrigerate until required.

Heat 1 tablespoon peanut oil in a large non-stick frying pan, add sweet potato and stir over high heat for 3-4 minutes or until just soft. Cool, then place in a bowl with green onions, shredded lime leaves, coriander, chillies and flour. Season to taste with sea salt and freshly ground black pepper and combine well. Add egg yolks and mix until well combined.

Using an electric mixer, whisk egg whites until soft peaks form, then gently fold into sweet potato mixture. Shape ¼ cupfuls into twelve 5cm rounds and coat with sesame seeds. Place on a baking paper-lined tray, cover and refrigerate for 2 hours.

Heat enough oil to cover the base of a large non-stick frying pan and cook fritters, in batches, adding more oil when necessary, until golden on both sides. Drain on absorbent paper.

Serve fritters immediately with avocado purée and rocket to the side.

**Serves 4 as a light meal or 6 as an entrée**

# Pea and pasta frittata with prosciutto

225g (1½ cups) podded peas, cooked until
    tender, then drained
100g dried thin egg fettuccine, coarsely broken,
    cooked until al dente, then drained
7 eggs, lightly beaten
40g (½ cup) grated pecorino
1 tablespoon chopped marjoram
Olive oil
200g sliced prosciutto, halved crosswise if large

Place peas, pasta, eggs, pecorino and marjoram in a large bowl, season to taste and stir until combined. Heat a 20cm heavy-based frying pan (preferably cast-iron) and, when very hot, add 2 tablespoons olive oil and swirl to coat base and side. Pour egg mixture into pan and cook over high heat for 2-3 minutes or until mixture is set on bottom and side, then, using a spatula, push cooked edge towards middle of pan, allowing uncooked mixture to run into the side and under base of frittata. Cook for another 2-3 minutes or until mixture is set around edges but still soft in the middle. Invert frittata onto a large plate, then slide back into pan and cook for another 3-4 minutes or until firm in the middle. Turn frittata onto a large plate and cool to room temperature.

Cut frittata into slices or wedges and wrap each piece in a slice of prosciutto, or serve prosciutto to the side.
Serves 6-8

# pasta + rice

Cooked in a flash and timeless in its simplicity, nothing could be easier than pasta…unless, of course, it is rice, transformed into a creamy risotto, a sweetly spiced pilaf or a filling kedgeree. Rice and pasta dishes never go out of favour and their variations are endless – just a few well-chosen additions (fish, herbs, vegetables, cheese), and quick, effortless cooking will yield stylish results.

## Spaghetti with toasted crumbs, anchovies, basil and pecorino

¼ cup extra virgin olive oil

6 anchovy fillets

100g (1½ cups) day-old breadcrumbs

1 clove of garlic, finely chopped

450g spaghetti

½ cup torn basil leaves

40g pecorino, grated

80g (½ cup) pitted kalamata olives, quartered

Heat olive oil in a non-stick frying pan, then add anchovies and stir over low-medium heat for 1 minute or until broken up. Add breadcrumbs and garlic and stir until breadcrumbs are golden.

Cook pasta in plenty of lightly salted boiling water until al dente, then drain and return to saucepan.

Add crumb mixture and basil to pasta and toss to combine. Season to taste with sea salt and freshly ground black pepper. Divide pasta among 4 bowls, top with pecorino and scatter with olives. Serve immediately.

Serves 4

# Ocean trout and mung bean kedgeree

2 tablespoons vegetable oil

2 tablespoons cumin seeds

2 dried bay leaves

1 stick of cinnamon

1 onion, finely chopped

110g (½ cup) split mung beans, soaked
in water for 3 hours, then drained

300g (1½ cups) basmati rice, soaked in
1 litre water for 30 minutes, then drained

¼ teaspoon each garam masala,
ground cardamom and ground cloves

¼ cup chopped coriander leaves,
plus extra, to serve

600g hot-smoked ocean trout,
flaked into large chunks

2 hard-boiled eggs, quartered

Mango chutney, to serve

Heat vegetable oil in a large heavy-based saucepan, add cumin seeds, bay leaves and cinnamon stick and cook over medium heat for 10 seconds or until cumin seeds begin to pop. Add onion and stir over low-medium heat until onion is soft, then add drained mung beans and rice and stir for 2 minutes or until well coated. Stir in garam masala, cardamom, cloves and coriander leaves and season to taste with sea salt and freshly ground black pepper. Add 600ml water and bring to the boil, stir well, cover and cook over low heat for 25 minutes or until rice is tender. Remove from heat and stand, covered, for 5 minutes. Discard cinnamon stick and bay leaves, then fluff rice with a fork and gently stir through flaked smoked ocean trout. Serve kedgeree topped with coriander sprigs and hard-boiled eggs, with mango chutney to the side.

**Serves 4**

# Asparagus and lemon risotto with zucchini

6 asparagus spears, trimmed and cut into 5cm pieces

2 small zucchini, trimmed and cut into 5mm-thick slices

2 tablespoons extra virgin olive oil

1 onion, finely chopped

400g (2 cups) arborio rice

125ml dry white wine

1.5 litres chicken or vegetable stock

Finely grated rind of 1 lemon

40g parmesan, grated

60g butter, chopped

Shaved parmesan, to serve

Cook asparagus and zucchini in boiling salted water for 1 minute, drain and cool under cold water, then drain again.

Heat olive oil in a large heavy-based saucepan, add onion and cook over low heat for 5 minutes or until soft. Add rice and stir over low heat until coated with oil and lightly toasted. Add wine and stir over medium heat until liquid is absorbed. Have stock simmering in another saucepan, then add 1 cup simmering stock to rice and stir over medium heat for 5 minutes or until stock is absorbed. Add remaining stock, ½ cup at a time, stirring continuously, allowing each addition to be absorbed before adding the next. When rice is al dente, stir in asparagus and zucchini with lemon rind, grated parmesan and butter, then season to taste with sea salt and freshly ground black pepper. Serve risotto scattered with shaved parmesan.

Serves 4

# Penne with tomato, cream, tuna and oregano sauce

2 tablespoons extra virgin olive oil

½ onion, finely chopped

1 small carrot, peeled and chopped

1 stalk of celery, chopped

400g can chopped tomatoes

¼ teaspoon caster sugar

4 sprigs of oregano

½ cup pouring cream

450g dried penne

2 x 185g cans tuna in olive oil, drained and flaked

1 tablespoon chopped oregano leaves, extra

Heat olive oil in a saucepan, add onion, carrot and celery and cook, stirring frequently, over medium heat for 8-10 minutes or until tender. Add tomatoes, sugar and oregano and season to taste, then cover and cook, stirring occasionally, over low heat for 30 minutes. Discard oregano and process tomato mixture in a food processor until smooth. Return tomato mixture to same pan, then stir in cream and cook over low heat until heated through.

Meanwhile, cook pasta in plenty of boiling salted water until al dente, drain, return pasta to pan, add tomato sauce and mix well. Gently stir in tuna, then divide among 4 bowls. Sprinkle with extra oregano leaves and serve immediately.

**Serves 4**

# Lamb pilaf with Middle Eastern spices

500g lamb backstraps, cut into 1cm pieces

1 teaspoon ground allspice

2 cloves of garlic, crushed

1 teaspoon grated ginger

2 tablespoons olive oil

1 tablespoon lemon juice

1 large onion, finely chopped

¼ teaspoon saffron threads, soaked in
   2 tablespoons hot water for 10 minutes

2 dried bay leaves

1 teaspoon each ground cardamom
   and ground cinnamon

½ teaspoon ground coriander

¼ teaspoon ground cloves

300g (1½ cups) basmati rice, soaked in 1 litre
   water for 30 minutes, then drained well

2 tablespoons currants

8 dried apricots, very thinly sliced

2¼ cups hot chicken stock

⅓ cup shredded mint leaves

35g (¼ cup) slivered pistachios, or coarsely
   chopped shelled pistachios

Minted yoghurt, to serve

Place lamb, allspice, half the garlic, grated ginger, 1 tablespoon olive oil and lemon juice in a glass or ceramic bowl and mix well, cover and refrigerate for 30 minutes or, if time permits, up to 2 hours.

Heat remaining olive oil in a large heavy-based saucepan and cook lamb, in batches, over high heat until browned. Remove lamb and set aside. Add onion to same pan and cook, covered, for 3-4 minutes or until soft. Add remaining garlic, saffron mixture, bay leaves and spices and cook for 30 seconds or until fragrant. Increase heat to high and stir in drained rice and lamb until well coated in spice mixture. Add currants and apricots and mix well, then pour in hot chicken stock and bring to the boil, season to taste and cook, covered, over low heat for 15-20 minutes or until liquid is absorbed and rice is tender. Stir in mint, scatter with pistachios and serve immediately with minted yoghurt.

Serves 4

# Mixed pea and prawn linguine

150g (1 cup) podded peas

100g sugarsnap peas, trimmed

100g snowpeas, trimmed

2 tablespoons olive oil

1 leek, thinly sliced

600g medium green prawns, shelled and cleaned

125ml dry white wine

½ cup pouring cream

¼ cup chervil sprigs

400g fresh linguine, cooked in boiling salted
   water until al dente, then drained

Cook peas in boiling water for 4 minutes, add sugarsnap peas and cook for 1 minute, then add snowpeas and cook for another 1 minute, then drain, refresh in iced water and drain again.

Heat olive oil in a deep, heavy-based frying pan, add leek and cook over low heat for 5 minutes or until soft. Add prawns and cook over medium-high heat for 2-3 minutes or until prawns change colour, add wine and cream and cook for another 1-2 minutes, then add all the peas and cook until heated through. Toss prawn mixture and chervil through pasta and season to taste. Serve immediately.

**Serves 4**

# Ravioli with fresh tomato, rocket, olive and caper sauce

3 small egg tomatoes, each cut into 6 wedges, then halved

80g baby rocket

2 green onions, thinly sliced

1 tablespoon torn basil leaves

1 tablespoon salted capers, soaked in water
for 15 minutes, then drained

75g kalamata olives, pitted and cut lengthways into slices

400g packet cheese or vegetable filled ravioli (see note)

¼ cup extra virgin olive oil

1 tablespoon aged balsamic vinegar

Ciabatta, optional, to serve

Place tomatoes, rocket, green onions, basil, capers and olives in a large bowl, then set aside.

Cook ravioli in boiling salted water until al dente, then drain well.

Drizzle tomato mixture with olive oil and balsamic vinegar and season to taste with sea salt and freshly ground black pepper, then add hot ravioli and toss gently to combine. Serve immediately, divided among bowls, with slices of ciabatta, if using.

**Serves 4 as an entrée or light lunch
or 2 as a main course**

Note: Pumpkin, potato, mixed cheese or spinach and ricotta ravioli, available from delicatessens or specialist pasta stores, are all suitable for use in this recipe.

# seafood

The briny savour and delicate texture of seafood just shine when cooked with a minimum of fuss: steaming, grilling, poaching, baking or frying are ideal techniques to use. Bright flavours (pungent herbs and spices, zingy citrus, salty capers) marry well with those of the sea, and the best accompaniments for seafood are all simple – rice, potatoes or salad.

## Steamed clams with vinegar and cured ham

1.5kg clams
1 tablespoon fine cornmeal or fine oatmeal
2 tablespoons olive oil
1 large onion, finely chopped
80g prosciutto, finely chopped
125ml dry white wine
½ cup torn flat-leaf parsley leaves
1 tablespoon sherry vinegar
Crusty bread, to serve

Rinse clams and place in a large bowl with enough lightly salted water to cover and sprinkle with cornmeal or oatmeal. Refrigerate for 3 hours or overnight (the clams will eat the meal and spit it out with any residual sand).

Heat olive oil in a large saucepan, add onion and prosciutto and stir occasionally over medium heat for 8 minutes or until golden. Add white wine, drained clams and half the parsley, bring to a simmer, then cover with a tight-fitting lid and steam over medium heat for 5 minutes or until clams open. Strain clams, reserving cooking liquid, and discard any unopened shells. Place clams in warm bowls. Return cooking liquid to saucepan and simmer for 1 minute, add vinegar and season to taste with cracked black pepper, then pour over clams. Scatter with remaining parsley and serve immediately with crusty bread.
**Serves 4 as an entrée or light lunch**

# Barbecued salmon with lemon couscous

6 salmon fillets (about 180g each), pin-boned

450g (2¼ cups) instant couscous

20g butter

3 green onions, thinly sliced

2 tablespoons finely chopped preserved lemon

Marinade

½ cup olive oil

2 tablespoons chopped coriander leaves

2 tablespoons chopped flat-leaf parsley leaves

1 teaspoon ground cumin

1 teaspoon dried chilli flakes

1 teaspoon ground turmeric

1 clove of garlic, finely chopped

Pinch of ground cinnamon

For marinade, stir all ingredients in a small bowl until well combined.

Place salmon fillets in a single layer in a large glass or ceramic dish, pour marinade over, turn to coat, then cover and refrigerate for 1-2 hours.

Combine couscous and butter in a heatproof bowl, add 1½ cups boiling water, mix well and stand, covered, for 10 minutes.

Meanwhile, remove salmon from marinade, then barbecue or char-grill salmon, skin-side down first and basting occasionally, for 3-4 minutes on each side for medium rare or until cooked to your liking.

Fluff couscous with a fork, add green onions and preserved lemon, season to taste and mix well. Serve salmon immediately with lemon couscous.

Serves 6

# Bay of Bengal fish curry

800g blue eye, skinned, pin-boned and cut into large chunks

1 teaspoon ground turmeric

2 onions, chopped

2 fresh long red chillies, seeded and chopped, optional

¾ cup (firmly packed) coriander leaves, plus extra, to serve

3 coriander roots and stems, washed

2cm piece of ginger, thinly sliced

2 cloves of garlic, crushed

2 tablespoons vegetable oil

1½ teaspoons black mustard seeds

1½ teaspoons each ground cumin, ground coriander, ground cardamom

1 teaspoon garam masala

¼ cup tamarind paste

400ml can coconut milk

Steamed basmati rice and lime wedges, to serve

Place fish in a single layer in a glass or ceramic dish, sprinkle evenly with turmeric and season to taste with sea salt, then cover and refrigerate for 10 minutes.

Meanwhile, process onions, chillies (if using), coriander leaves, roots and stems, ginger and garlic in a food processor until a smooth paste forms.

Heat oil in a large saucepan, add paste and fry, stirring frequently, over medium heat for 5 minutes or until fragrant. Add mustard seeds, ground spices and garam masala and fry for 2-3 minutes. Add tamarind paste, coconut milk and 190ml water, then bring to a simmer and cook for 5 minutes. Add fish pieces and stir to coat in sauce, then simmer over medium heat for 10-15 minutes or until fish is just cooked through. Season to taste with sea salt, scatter with extra coriander leaves and serve with steamed rice and lime wedges.

Serves 4-6

# Baked fish with almond sauce

6 silver bream (about 350g each), cleaned

¾ cup coarsely chopped flat-leaf parsley

½ cup coarsely chopped dill

Extra virgin olive oil

Steamed basmati rice, to serve

Orange, lemon and onion salad (recipe follows), to serve

Almond sauce

160g (1 cup) whole blanched almonds

1 slice day-old bread, crusts removed, soaked in water
    for 1 minute and squeezed dry

1 clove of garlic, finely chopped

½ teaspoon ground cinnamon

¼ cup verjuice or white wine vinegar

¼ cup olive oil

For almond sauce, process almonds, bread, garlic and cinnamon in a food processor until mixture is very finely chopped. With motor running, add verjuice, olive oil and ½ cup water and process until mixture forms a paste. Season to taste with sea salt and freshly ground black pepper.

Make 3 deep cuts in both sides of each fish. Combine parsley and dill and fill each cut with herb mixture, then place remaining mixture in cavities and season fish to taste. Place fish in a single layer in a well-oiled roasting dish, drizzle liberally with extra virgin olive oil and roast at 200C for 8-10 minutes or until just cooked through.

Serve fish with almond sauce, steamed basmati rice, and orange, lemon and onion salad.

Serves 6

## Orange, lemon and onion salad

4 oranges, peeled and pith removed, thinly sliced

1 lemon, peeled and pith removed, thinly sliced

1 spanish onion, thinly sliced into rings

2 tablespoons salted capers, soaked in cold water
    for 1 hour, then drained

¼ cup extra virgin olive oil

Combine orange and lemon slices, onion and capers in a large bowl. Season to taste with sea salt and freshly ground black pepper, toss gently, then drizzle with olive oil.

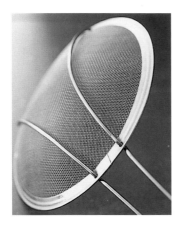

# Salt and pepper squid

1kg cleaned small squid hoods

2 tablespoons lemon juice

2½ teaspoons sea salt, plus extra for sprinkling

1½ teaspoons black peppercorns, roasted

1½ teaspoons ground white pepper

3 teaspoons sichuan pepper, roasted

75g (½ cup) plain flour

35g (¼ cup) rice flour

Peanut oil, for deep-frying

2 egg whites, lightly beaten

Steamed jasmine rice, to serve

Salad plate

1 lebanese cucumber, thinly sliced lengthways
   with a vegetable peeler

100g (1¼ cups) beansprouts

1 cup coriander sprigs

6 green onions, shredded

Cut through squid hoods on one side, open out flat and, using a sharp knife, cut shallow diagonal slashes in a criss-cross pattern on inside surface of squid, then cut into 3x4cm pieces. Toss squid with lemon juice, cover and refrigerate for 15 minutes.

For salad plate, divide vegetables and herbs among 4 plates.

Combine sea salt, peppercorns and peppers in a mortar or spice grinder and grind (with a pestle, if using) until fine, transfer to a bowl and stir in flours until well combined.

Drain squid and pat dry with absorbent paper. Fill a deep heavy-based saucepan one-third full with peanut oil and heat to 180C, or until a cube of bread browns in 15 seconds. Coat squid pieces first in egg white, then in flour mixture, and deep-fry, in batches, for 1 minute or until light golden and cooked through, then drain on absorbent paper.

Serve immediately, sprinkled with extra salt and freshly ground black pepper, with salad plate and steamed rice passed separately.

Serves 4

# Prawns with three sauces

In cooler weather, serve the prawns warm. In summer, refresh prawns in a bowl of iced water and serve at room temperature.

1kg medium green prawns
Crusty bread and a salad, to serve

Cook prawns in boiling salted water for 1–2 minutes or until pink. Using a slotted spoon, remove from water and drain well.
Serves 4

## Tarragon and caper mayonnaise

1 cup whole egg mayonnaise
1½ tablespoons finely chopped capers
2 tablespoons finely chopped tarragon
2 tablespoons lemon juice
1 teaspoon Dijon mustard

Combine all ingredients in a bowl, season to taste with freshly ground black pepper and mix well.
Makes about 1½ cups

## Red capsicum and chilli sauce

1 red capsicum, grilled until skin blackens, peeled and chopped
½ cup crème fraîche
2 teaspoons Worcestershire sauce
2 teaspoons sweet chilli sauce

Process red capsicum in a food processor until smooth. Add remaining ingredients and, using the pulse button, process until just combined. Season to taste with sea salt and freshly ground black pepper and mix well.
Makes about 1 cup

## Toasted breadcrumb and parsley sauce

1 cup olive oil
2 tablespoons red wine vinegar
2 tablespoons lemon juice
2 cloves of garlic, crushed
2 tablespoons finely chopped flat-leaf parsley leaves
50g (⅔ cup) day-old breadcrumbs, dried in oven until crisp

Combine olive oil, vinegar, lemon juice, garlic and parsley in a small bowl and whisk until well combined. Just before serving add breadcrumbs, season to taste and mix well.
Makes about 1½ cups

# Gremolata-crumbed whiting with warm baked potato salad

¼ cup flat-leaf parsley leaves, chopped

Grated rind of 1 lemon

210g (3 cups) day-old breadcrumbs, dried in oven until crisp

2 teaspoons capers, drained and chopped

12 whiting fillets (about 50g each)

75g (½ cup) plain flour

1 egg, lightly beaten with 1 tablespoon water

Vegetable oil, for shallow-frying

Lemon wedges, to serve

Dressing

2 tablespoons sour cream

2 tablespoons mayonnaise

1 tablespoon Dijon mustard

Warm baked potato salad

800g chat potatoes, halved

2 tablespoons extra virgin olive oil

1 small spanish onion, thinly sliced

2 tablespoons chopped flat-leaf parsley leaves

1 tablespoon chopped sage leaves

For dressing, whisk all ingredients with 1 tablespoon water in a small bowl until well combined, then season to taste.

For warm baked potato salad, place potatoes in a roasting tray, drizzle with olive oil, season to taste and toss gently to combine. Bake potatoes at 200C for 20 minutes, then add onion, toss to combine and bake for another 10-15 minutes or until vegetables are cooked. Just before serving, toss potato mixture with dressing, then gently stir herbs through.

Meanwhile, combine parsley, lemon rind, breadcrumbs and capers in a shallow bowl and season to taste. Dust whiting fillets in flour, shaking away excess, and dip in egg mixture, then coat in breadcrumb mixture, pressing crumbs onto fish to coat evenly. Shallow-fry crumbed fillets, in batches, in hot vegetable oil for 2 minutes each side or until golden and just cooked, then drain on absorbent paper. Serve crumbed whiting immediately with warm baked potato salad and lemon wedges to the side.

**Serves 4**

# Vietnamese caramel-glazed salmon

2 tablespoons vegetable oil

1 clove of garlic, bruised with the back of a knife

90g (⅓ cup) grated dark palm sugar

2 tablespoons fish sauce

2 tablespoons rice vinegar

4 salmon fillets (about 180-200g each), pin-boned

50g watercress sprigs

50g snowpea sprouts

Steamed rice and lime wedges, to serve

Dressing

3 teaspoons vegetable oil

2 teaspoons rice vinegar

2 teaspoons lime juice

1 teaspoon light soy sauce

For dressing, combine oil, rice vinegar, lime juice, soy sauce and 2 teaspoons warm water in a small bowl and mix well.

Heat 1 tablespoon vegetable oil in a small saucepan, add garlic and cook until fragrant. Remove and discard garlic, then add palm sugar, fish sauce, rice vinegar and ½ cup water. Bring to the boil and simmer for 15 minutes or until syrupy. Remove from heat and leave to cool.

Brush salmon lightly with remaining oil and season to taste, then heat a large non-stick frying pan until hot, add salmon, skin-side down, and cook over medium heat for 1-2 minutes or until skin is crisp, then turn and cook for another 1-2 minutes for medium rare or until cooked to your liking. When salmon is almost cooked, reduce heat to low, add palm sugar mixture and quickly turn salmon to coat, taking care not to burn the glaze. Divide fish and sauce among plates. Combine dressing with watercress and snowpea sprouts and toss gently to combine. Serve fish, topped with watercress and snowpea sprouts, with steamed rice and lime wedges.

**Serves 4**

# Fennel and seafood stew with bruschetta

2 tablespoons olive oil

2 onions, finely chopped

1 clove of garlic, finely chopped

3 cups fish stock

250ml dry white wine

400g can whole peeled tomatoes

2 sprigs of oregano

2 bulbs of fennel, trimmed (reserving leaves),
    cored and thinly sliced

½ teaspoon dried chilli flakes

300g small black mussels, scrubbed and bearded

500g boneless white fish fillets, cut into large chunks

500g medium green prawns, shelled and cleaned,
    leaving tails intact

1 tablespoon chopped flat-leaf parsley

Bruschetta

8 slices sourdough bread

Extra virgin olive oil

2 cloves of garlic, halved

For bruschetta, brush bread on both sides with extra virgin olive oil, grill under a hot grill until golden on both sides, then rub slices with halved cloves of garlic.

Heat olive oil in a large saucepan, add onions and garlic and cook over medium heat for 5-8 minutes or until soft. Stir in stock, wine, tomatoes and their juices and oregano and bring to the boil. Add fennel, chilli flakes and salt to taste and simmer, covered, over low-medium heat for 10 minutes or until fennel is tender. Add mussels and cook, covered, for 2-4 minutes or until mussels open, then remove with a slotted spoon, discarding any unopened mussels. Add fish and prawns to tomato mixture and cook, covered, for about 2 minutes or until prawns just change colour. Return mussels to pan, sprinkle with 2 tablespoons chopped reserved fennel leaves and parsley, then adjust seasoning to taste and serve immediately with bruschetta.

Serves 4

# Marinated red mullet grilled in vine leaves

½ cup extra virgin olive oil

½ cup orange juice

100ml ouzo

2 teaspoons finely grated orange rind

2 cloves of garlic, finely chopped

1 teaspoon dried oregano

12 red mullet (about 1kg), cleaned

Vine leaves in brine, rinsed and drained

Olive oil

Roast potatoes, olives and rocket
   salad, optional, to serve

Combine extra virgin olive oil, orange juice, ouzo, orange rind, garlic and oregano in a small bowl and whisk until well combined. Place fish in a glass or ceramic dish, pour ouzo mixture over, cover with plastic wrap and refrigerate for 4 hours.

Drain fish well, discarding marinade, and season to taste with sea salt and freshly ground black pepper. Wrap each fish tightly in 1-2 vine leaves, depending on size, then brush wrapped fish all over with olive oil. Heat a barbecue or char-grill pan and, when hot, char-grill fish, in batches, for 2-3 minutes on each side or until just cooked. Serve red mullet with roast potatoes, olives and rocket salad, if using.

**Serves 4 as a light lunch or dinner**

# Piri piri prawns with saffron and almond rice

1kg medium green prawns

Piri piri sauce

9 fresh long red chillies (about 12cm long)

3 cloves of garlic, crushed

75ml white wine vinegar

¾ cup olive oil

Saffron and almond rice

Pinch of saffron threads

80ml dry white wine

Olive oil

125g blanched whole almonds

1 large onion, finely chopped

200g (1 cup) long-grain rice, rinsed well and drained

½ cup flat-leaf parsley leaves, thickly shredded

For piri piri sauce, place chillies on an oven tray and cook under a hot grill until blistered and blackened. When cool enough to handle, rub skin from chillies and remove stalks. Process garlic and chilli (with seeds) in a food processor until finely chopped, add remaining ingredients and process until well combined.

Using a small sharp knife or scissors, carefully cut through back of each prawn shell, remove vein and open shell slightly to expose flesh. Place prawns in a glass or ceramic dish, add three-quarters of the piri piri sauce and stir to coat well, then cover and refrigerate for 2 hours or overnight. Note that the chilli heat intensifies the longer the prawns marinate.

For saffron and almond rice, combine saffron and white wine in a small cup and stand for 10 minutes. Heat ⅓ cup olive oil in a saucepan, add almonds and stir over medium heat until dark golden, then remove with a slotted spoon and drain on absorbent paper. Add onion to same pan and cook over medium heat for 8 minutes or until soft, then add rice and stir until lightly toasted. Add wine and saffron mixture to rice, cook until liquid has nearly evaporated, then add 1½ cups water and 1 teaspoon sea salt and bring to the boil, cover with a tight-fitting lid and cook over low heat for 12 minutes. Remove from heat and stand, covered, for 5 minutes, then stir in almonds, parsley and 1 tablespoon olive oil.

Meanwhile, barbecue or char-grill drained prawns, in batches, over medium-high heat for 1 minute each side or until shells turn bright orange.

Serve prawns with saffron and almond rice, with remaining piri piri sauce passed separately.

Serves 4-6

# meat

Prime cuts that cook in a flash need little embellishment…a rubbing with herbs or a rich spice paste, a light dusting with crumbs, or a finishing spoonful of horseradish-spiked sauce. Deeply flavoured braises, redolent of wine, aromatics and meaty stocks, virtually cook by themselves, making them the most simple of dishes to produce.

## Barbecued pork fillets with beetroot, bay and onion kebabs

¼ cup chopped rosemary

4 cloves of garlic, crushed

2 tablespoons lemon juice

Extra virgin olive oil

1 tablespoon finely grated lemon rind

3 pork fillets (about 250g each)

Lemon halves, to serve

Baby endive salad, to serve

Beetroot, bay and onion kebabs

18 baby beetroot, washed and trimmed

18 small pickling onions,
    unpeeled, trimmed

36 large fresh bay leaves, soaked in cold
    water for 2 hours, then drained

6 metal skewers, or bamboo skewers
    soaked in warm water for 30 minutes

¼ cup extra virgin olive oil

1 tablespoon balsamic or sherry vinegar

Process rosemary and garlic in the small bowl of a food processor, or pound in a mortar with a pestle until coarsely ground, then add lemon juice and 2 tablespoons olive oil and process or pound until a paste forms. Stir in lemon rind and season to taste. Place pork fillets in a glass or ceramic dish, spread ¾ of the paste over and rub in well. Char-grill or barbecue pork fillets, brushing with remaining paste, for 5-6 minutes each side or until cooked through, then rest in a warm place for 5 minutes.

For beetroot, bay and onion kebabs, blanch beetroot and onions, separately, in lightly salted boiling water for 5 minutes, then drain and refresh under cold water. Pat dry with absorbent paper and peel onions.

Thread beetroot, onions and damp bay leaves onto skewers, alternating vegetables as you go. Drizzle with olive oil and vinegar and season to taste. Barbecue skewers for 20-25 minutes, turning occasionally, until charred and tender.

Serve sliced pork with beetroot, bay and onion kebabs and lemon halves, with endive salad to the side.

Serves 6

# Skirt steak with vinegar glaze and sweet and sour pears

3 teaspoons rosemary leaves

2 cloves of garlic

Olive oil

60ml red wine

1.2kg beef skirt steak, trimmed of sinew

⅓ cup balsamic vinegar

2 tablespoons brown sugar

Steamed chat potatoes and green beans, to serve

Sweet and sour pears

175g sun-dried pear halves, quartered

75ml red wine vinegar

55g (¼ cup) caster sugar

Large pinch of ground cinnamon

2 star anise

For sweet and sour pears, combine all ingredients and 1 cup water in a heavy-based saucepan and stir over medium heat until sugar dissolves, then simmer over medium heat for 10-15 minutes or until most of the liquid has been absorbed and pears are tender. Season to taste and cool to room temperature.

Combine 2 teaspoons rosemary leaves, garlic and freshly ground black pepper to taste in a mortar and crush with a pestle, gradually add ¼ cup olive oil and red wine and stir until well combined. Score membrane side of steak and place in a glass or ceramic dish. Drizzle with herb mixture, turn to coat, then cover and refrigerate for 4 hours or overnight.

Drain steak from marinade and discard marinade. Combine balsamic vinegar, sugar and remaining rosemary in a small bowl. Brush steak with vinegar mixture and char-grill or barbecue, scored-side down first, for 8-10 minutes on each side, basting frequently. Rest steak, covered, in a warm place for 10 minutes, then slice against the grain. Serve steak with a spoonful of sweet and sour pears, steamed chat potatoes and green beans.

**Makes about 1¼ cups sweet and sour pears**

**Serves 6-8**

# Veal piccata

4 veal schnitzels (about 600g), halved if large
Plain flour, seasoned to taste, for dusting
2 egg yolks, lightly beaten
1 cup milk
140g (2 cups) day-old sourdough breadcrumbs
2 tablespoons olive oil
60g butter
2 cloves of garlic, thinly sliced
2 teaspoons plain flour, extra
60ml dry white wine
¼ cup verjuice
⅓ cup beef stock
2 tablespoons salted baby capers, well rinsed
2 tablespoons chopped flat-leaf parsley
Steamed chat potatoes and a green salad, to serve

Lightly dust veal with flour, shaking away excess, dip into combined egg yolk and milk mixture, then coat with sourdough breadcrumbs, pressing crumbs onto veal to coat evenly.

Heat 1 tablespoon olive oil and 20g butter in a large heavy-based frying pan over medium-high heat and cook veal, in batches, for 2 minutes on each side or until lightly browned. Remove from pan and set aside in a warm place.

In a clean frying pan, heat remaining olive oil and 20g butter, add garlic and stir over low heat for 3 minutes or until softened. Stir in extra flour, add wine and whisk until mixture thickens, then simmer until reduced by half. Add verjuice, stock and capers and simmer over medium heat for 5 minutes, then remove from heat and whisk in remaining butter and parsley and season to taste.

Serve veal piccata drizzled with sauce, with steamed chat potatoes and a green salad.

Serves 4

# Lamb shanks with green olives and anchovy served on soft polenta

¼ cup olive oil

4 lamb shanks (about 300g each),
    french-trimmed

4 cloves of garlic, crushed

8 anchovies

2 tablespoons plain flour

2 tablespoons tomato paste

500ml red wine

1 cup chicken stock

100g queen (jumbo) green olives

Flat-leaf parsley sprigs, to serve

Soft polenta

2 cups milk

150g instant polenta

40g (½ cup) grated parmesan

20g butter

Heat olive oil in a large heavy-based flameproof casserole, add lamb shanks and cook over high heat until browned all over. Remove and set aside. Reduce heat to low-medium, add garlic and anchovies and stir until anchovies form a paste. Add flour and tomato paste and stir for 3 minutes, then add red wine and boil for 5 minutes. Return shanks to pan with chicken stock and olives, then cover and cook in oven at 180C for 2 hours or until meat is nearly falling off the bone.

For soft polenta, 5 minutes before shanks are ready, combine milk with 2 cups water in a heavy-based saucepan and bring to the boil. Whisk in polenta in a steady stream, then stir over medium heat for 3-5 minutes or until mixture is thick. Remove from heat, stir in parmesan and butter and season to taste. Serve lamb shanks on a bed of soft polenta with sauce spooned over and topped with parsley.

Serves 4

# Braised chicken with pinenut couscous

1.8kg organic chicken, cut into 8

1½ teaspoons ground cumin

2 tablespoons vegetable oil

1 spanish onion, finely chopped

3 cloves of garlic, crushed

Pinch of saffron threads, soaked in 1 tablespoon hot water

3 coriander roots with stems, washed well and finely chopped

2½ tablespoons ras el hanout

2½ cups hot chicken stock

200g fresh dates, pitted and halved

Chopped coriander leaves and harissa, to serve

Pinenut couscous

400g (2 cups) instant couscous

20g butter

2 cups boiling chicken stock

¼ cup chopped fresh coriander leaves

80g (½ cup) pinenuts

Sprinkle chicken with ½ teaspoon ground cumin. Heat oil in a large flameproof casserole and brown chicken pieces, in batches, over medium heat, then remove and set aside. Add onion, garlic, saffron mixture and coriander roots to same pan and cook for 5 minutes or until soft. Add remaining cumin and ras el hanout and cook for 1 minute or until fragrant. Return chicken to pan and stir to coat in spice mixture. Add hot chicken stock, bring to a simmer and cook, covered, over low heat for 1¼ hours or until chicken is tender. Stir in dates and cook, covered, for another 5 minutes.

Meanwhile, for pinenut couscous, place couscous and butter in a heatproof bowl, add boiling stock and stir well, then cover and stand for 10 minutes or until liquid is absorbed. Using a fork, fluff couscous to separate grains, then stir in coriander and pinenuts, season to taste and mix well.

Serve braised chicken and dates with sauce spooned over, scattered with chopped coriander leaves, with pinenut couscous and harissa.

Serves 4

## Sausages braised with white beans

4 thick Italian-style sausages (about 600g)

2 tablespoons olive oil

1 onion, finely chopped

3 cloves of garlic, crushed

1 large bulb of fennel, trimmed and finely chopped

½ teaspoon dried chilli flakes

1 tablespoon tomato paste

400g can chopped tomatoes

440g can cannellini beans, drained and rinsed

½ cup chicken stock

1 small sprig of rosemary

2 tablespoons chopped flat-leaf parsley leaves

Shaved parmesan and slices of Italian-style bread,
    brushed with olive oil, grilled and rubbed with
    a clove of garlic, to serve

Place sausages in a saucepan of cold water and bring to the boil, reduce heat to medium and simmer for 2 minutes, then drain well. When cool, cut on the diagonal into 2cm pieces.

Heat olive oil in a heavy-based flameproof casserole, add sausage pieces and cook over medium-high heat until browned, then drain on absorbent paper. Reduce heat to low-medium, then add onion, garlic, fennel and chilli to pan and cook, stirring occasionally, for 20 minutes or until soft, then stir in tomato paste and cook for another 5 minutes. Add sausages, tomatoes, beans, stock and rosemary, cover and cook over low heat for 20 minutes. Stir in parsley and season to taste. Serve braised sausages and white beans topped with shaved parmesan and with slices of garlic toast.

**Serves 4**

# Chicken fricassee

1 tablespoon olive oil

20g butter

12 cloves of garlic, peeled

12 shallots, peeled

1.6kg chicken, cut into 8 pieces on the bone

1 tablespoon plain flour

125ml white wine

4 sprigs of thyme

½ cup chicken stock

1 tablespoon lemon juice

2 egg yolks

1 tablespoon pouring cream

2 tablespoons chopped flat-leaf parsley leaves

Buttered fettuccine and a green salad, to serve

Heat olive oil and butter in a heavy-based flameproof casserole, large enough to fit chicken in a single layer, over low-medium heat. Add garlic and shallots and cook, stirring frequently, for 10-15 minutes or until golden and softened. Using a slotted spoon, remove vegetables from pan and set aside. Add chicken pieces to same pan and cook, without browning, until sealed, then remove and set aside.

Stir flour into pan juices and cook for 1 minute, then stir in white wine and simmer until reduced by half. Add thyme and chicken stock and bring to a simmer. Return chicken, except breast pieces, to pan with garlic and shallots, reduce heat to low and cook, covered, for 45 minutes. Add chicken breast pieces and cook, covered, for another 15 minutes. Remove chicken pieces and set aside.

Increase heat to medium and boil sauce for 10 minutes or until reduced and thickened. Meanwhile, whisk together lemon juice, egg yolks and cream in a small bowl until just combined. Remove pan from heat and, while whisking sauce, slowly pour in egg mixture until well combined. Add parsley and season to taste, then return chicken to pan and stir to coat with sauce. Serve chicken fricassee with buttered fettuccine and a green salad.

Serves 4-6

# Pork chops with roasted pear and potato

2 tablespoons lemon juice

2 teaspoons Dijon mustard, plus extra, to serve

3 cloves of garlic, crushed

2 tablespoons chopped flat-leaf parsley leaves

Olive oil

4 pork loin chops (about 250g each)

4 ripe but firm small beurre bosc pears,
    quartered and cored

500g kipfler potatoes, scrubbed and sliced

40g butter, finely chopped

25g (⅓ cup) grated parmesan

Combine lemon juice, mustard, garlic, parsley and 2 tablespoons olive oil in a glass or ceramic dish. Add pork chops and turn to coat, then cover and refrigerate for at least 1 hour.

Combine pears, potatoes and butter in an ovenproof dish, drizzle with 1 tablespoon olive oil and season to taste with sea salt and freshly ground black pepper, then toss until well combined. Roast at 180C, stirring occasionally, for 40-50 minutes or until golden.

Heat a lightly oiled heavy-based frying pan over medium-high heat, add pork and cook for 1-2 minutes on each side until browned, then place pork and any cooking juices over potato mixture in dish and cook at 180C for 5-10 minutes or until pork is cooked through. Remove pork and rest for 5 minutes before serving with roasted pears and potatoes, sprinkled with parmesan.

**Serves 4**

# Barbecued leg of lamb with Indian spices and yoghurt

2kg easy carve leg of lamb, untied and unrolled

Lime pickle, steamed basmati rice and naan bread, to serve

Indian spice mix

1 tablespoon coriander seeds

1 teaspoon cumin seeds

½ teaspoon yellow mustard seeds

1 cardamom pod, seeds removed

½ teaspoon ground turmeric

½cm piece of cinnamon stick

¼ teaspoon ground cloves

¼ teaspoon chilli flakes

½ teaspoon black peppercorns

1 cup Greek-style yoghurt

2 tablespoons lemon juice

2 cloves of garlic, crushed

1 teaspoon grated ginger

For Indian spice mix, combine coriander, cumin, mustard and cardamom seeds in a small non-stick frying pan and cook over low heat for 1 minute or until fragrant. Combine toasted spices with turmeric, cinnamon, cloves, chilli flakes and peppercorns in a mortar or spice grinder and grind (with a pestle, if using) until a powder forms. Transfer spice mixture to a small bowl and stir in remaining ingredients.

Place lamb in a glass or ceramic dish and rub all over with spice mixture, cover and refrigerate for at least 2 hours or overnight.

Barbecue lamb, covered, for 1 hour for medium rare or until cooked to your liking. Alternatively, place lamb over a roasting rack in a roasting pan and roast at 200C for 1 hour for medium rare or until cooked to your liking. Remove and rest, covered loosely with foil, for 10 minutes. Serve sliced with lime pickle, steamed basmati rice and naan bread.

Serves 4-6

# Fillet of beef with horseradish crème fraîche and glazed parsnips

4 large parsnips, peeled and trimmed (about 720g)

20g butter

1 tablespoon olive oil

2 tablespoons brown sugar

1 clove of garlic, crushed

⅓ cup crème fraîche

1 tablespoon horseradish cream

2 teaspoons Dijon mustard

1 tablespoon finely shredded sage

4 beef fillet steaks (about 200g each)

Watercress salad, to serve

Cut parsnips lengthways into quarters, cook in boiling salted water for 5 minutes, then drain and set aside. Melt butter in a flameproof roasting dish, add olive oil, sugar and garlic and stir until well combined. Remove from heat, add parsnips and toss until well combined, then season to taste. Roast at 200C, turning frequently to coat with glaze, for 40-50 minutes or until golden and tender.

Combine crème fraîche, horseradish cream, mustard and sage in a small bowl, season to taste and set aside.

Char-grill or barbecue steaks for 3-5 minutes on each side for medium rare or until cooked to your liking, then rest, covered, in a warm place for 5 minutes. Serve steaks topped with a spoonful of crème fraîche mixture, with glazed parsnips and watercress salad to the side.

Serves 4

# Chicken with orzo, tomato, zucchini and mint

¼ cup extra virgin olive oil

1kg chicken thigh fillets, fat removed, halved

2 zucchini, thickly sliced

2 leeks, washed well and thinly sliced

6 egg tomatoes, coarsely chopped

300g (1⅓ cups) orzo

160g (1⅓ cups) large green olives

2 cups chicken stock

⅓ cup torn mint leaves

Heat 2 tablespoons olive oil in a large heavy-based casserole and brown chicken, in batches, over medium heat, then drain on absorbent paper. Add remaining olive oil, zucchini and leeks and cook over medium heat for 5 minutes or until lightly browned. Add tomatoes and cook for 1 minute, then add orzo, olives and chicken stock and bring to the boil. Add chicken and stir well, then cover with tight-fitting lid and simmer gently, stirring occasionally, over medium heat for 10 minutes. Remove from heat and stand for 5 minutes. Season to taste, stir in mint, then spoon into shallow bowls and serve immediately.

Serves 4-6

# desserts

There's nothing quite like the promise of a homemade dessert. The simpler puddings are often the most loved and these demand little dressing up. A quick drizzle with syrup, a shower of sugar, some dollops of luscious cream, or a scattering of juicy berries give that special finishing touch to easy, sweet endings.

## Sweet baked ricotta with strawberry sauce

75g (⅓ cup) caster sugar
⅓ cup sweet orange marmalade
1kg ricotta
1 teaspoon vanilla extract
Grated rind of 1 orange
50ml brandy
4 eggs, lightly beaten
35g (¼ cup) plain flour, sifted
Icing sugar, for dusting
Strawberry sauce
75g (⅓ cup) caster sugar
80ml red wine
⅓ cup orange juice
500g strawberries, hulled and sliced

Process sugar and marmalade in a food processor until smooth, then add ricotta, vanilla, orange rind, brandy and eggs and process until mixture is well combined and smooth. Stir in flour. Pour mixture into a lightly greased and floured 18cm springform pan and bake for 1 hour at 170C (it will still be slightly wobbly in the centre), then turn oven off and leave baked ricotta in oven, with oven door slightly ajar, until cool.

For strawberry sauce, combine sugar, wine and juice in a saucepan and stir over medium heat for 3 minutes or until sugar dissolves. Add berries and cook until berries are soft. Process mixture in a food processor until smooth, then return to saucepan and simmer over medium heat, skimming any scum that rises to the surface, until mixture has reduced enough to coat the back of a spoon. Cool.

Serve baked ricotta at room temperature or lightly chilled, dusted with icing sugar, with strawberry sauce.
Serves 8

# Rice-flour pudding with saffron-poached apricots

3¼ cups milk

⅓ cup honey

6 cardamom pods, crushed

2 5cm-long strips orange rind

75g (½ cup) rice flour

1 tablespoon cornflour

1 tablespoon orange flower water

Saffron-poached apricots

150g dried apricots

¼ teaspoon saffron threads

75g (⅓ cup) caster sugar

For saffron-poached apricots, place apricots in a small bowl, pour 1¼ cups boiling water over and sprinkle with saffron. Stand for 2 hours or overnight, then combine in a saucepan with sugar and bring to a simmer. Cook over low heat for 30 minutes or until apricots are tender, then cool.

Combine milk, honey, cardamom and rind in a small saucepan and slowly bring to a simmer. Remove from heat and stand for 20 minutes for flavours to develop, then strain mixture, discarding solids, and return liquid to saucepan.

Combine rice flour and cornflour with enough infused milk to make a smooth paste. Return milk to heat, bring to a simmer and pour in the rice-flour mixture, whisking continuously, then stir over low heat until mixture is smooth and thick. Remove from heat, stir in orange flower water, cool slightly, then divide rice-flour pudding among 6 small glasses or dishes. Cool to room temperature, then refrigerate before serving topped with saffron-poached apricots.

**Serves 6**

# Milk, honey and vanilla jelly with raspberries in vanilla syrup

2¾ cups milk

¾ cup pouring cream

½ cup floral honey

2 vanilla beans

7½ teaspoons powdered gelatine

Raspberries in vanilla syrup

110g (½ cup) caster sugar

1 vanilla bean, split lengthways

220g raspberries

Combine milk, cream, honey and vanilla beans in a heavy-based saucepan and, over low heat, very slowly bring mixture just to the boil, then remove from heat.

Meanwhile, place ⅓ cup water in a small heatproof cup or bowl and sprinkle powdered gelatine over. Place cup in a small saucepan of simmering water and stir until gelatine dissolves, then combine with milk mixture and cool to room temperature. Remove vanilla beans and reserve for another recipe.

Strain mixture through a fine sieve into a lightly oiled 20.5cm-diameter, 9cm-deep, 5-cup-capacity brioche tin or six individual ¾-cup-capacity greased metal moulds, then refrigerate overnight until set.

For raspberries in vanilla syrup, combine sugar, scraped seeds from vanilla bean and bean, with 1 cup water in a saucepan and stir over medium heat until sugar dissolves, then bring to the boil. Add raspberries and cook for 1 minute, then remove from heat and cool to room temperature.

Dip base of jelly in a bowl of warm water for 10 seconds, then, using a finger, gently push jelly from side of tin. Place a plate with raised sides over the top and shake firmly to release jelly from mould, then carefully lift tin away from jelly. Drizzle jelly with syrup and spoon raspberries around.

**Serves 6**

# Lemon sago pudding

100g (½ cup) sago
165g (¾ cup) caster sugar
Grated rind of 3 lemons
½ cup lemon juice
1 tablespoon golden syrup
Whipped cream, optional, to serve

Combine sago, sugar, lemon rind and 3 cups water in a saucepan and bring to a gentle simmer. Stir regularly over low-medium heat for 20 minutes or until sago is translucent and soft and mixture is thick. Remove from heat, stir in lemon juice and golden syrup and cool for 30 minutes. Serve warm with whipped cream, if using.
Serves 6

# Rhubarb and rosewater clafoutis

600g trimmed rhubarb, cut into 2-3cm pieces

150g (⅔ cup) caster sugar

2 teaspoons lemon juice

4 eggs, lightly whisked

2 egg yolks

150g (⅔ cup) caster sugar, extra

75g (½ cup) plain flour

200ml milk

200ml pouring cream

½ teaspoon rosewater, or to taste

Combine rhubarb, sugar and lemon juice in a frying pan, stir over low heat until sugar is almost dissolved, then cook, covered, for another 3-5 minutes or until just tender. Strain rhubarb, reserving cooking liquid.

Whisk eggs, egg yolks and 100g extra sugar until well combined, then whisk in flour until smooth. Add milk, cream and rosewater and whisk until well combined.

Divide rhubarb among 8 shallow 1¼-cup-capacity greased ovenproof dishes and pour batter over, then place dishes on an oven tray and bake at 190C for 15 minutes or until just set. Boil reserved cooking juices until syrupy, then drizzle over clafoutis. Serve hot or at room temperature, sprinkled with remaining sugar.

**Serves 8**

# Little chocolate mud cakes

110g (¾ cup) plain flour

¼ teaspoon baking powder

2 tablespoons cocoa, plus extra, for dusting

125g butter, chopped

75g dark chocolate, chopped

220g (1 cup) caster sugar

2 tablespoons Tia Maria or other coffee-flavoured liqueur

1 egg, lightly beaten

Strawberries and thick cream, optional, to serve

Sift flour, baking powder and cocoa together into a large bowl.

Combine butter, chocolate, sugar, liqueur and ½ cup hot water in a small saucepan and stir over low heat until chocolate melts and mixture is well combined. Cool for 5 minutes, then stir chocolate mixture into flour mixture with egg until just smooth. Divide mixture evenly among six holes of a greased muffin pan or six 150ml-capacity greased ovenproof dishes and bake at 160C for 30 minutes or until cakes are firm to touch. Stand cakes in tin for 5 minutes before turning out onto a wire rack to cool.

Serve cakes dusted with extra cocoa powder and strawberries and cream passed separately, if using. Cakes will keep in an airtight container for up to 2 days.

**Makes 6**

# Crumbly cake

From the Lombardy region of Italy, *torta sbrisolona*, or crumbly cake, is so named because of its compact and fairly dry texture. Serve simply with a cup of tea or coffee or as a dessert with mascarpone and berries cooked in syrup.

250g (1⅔ cups) unbleached plain flour

200g fine cornmeal

140g blanched whole almonds, roasted and finely chopped

200g caster sugar

125g butter, finely chopped

½ cup vegetable oil

3 eggs, lightly beaten

1 tablespoon vanilla extract

1 tablespoon finely grated lemon rind

Icing sugar, for dusting

Combine flour, cornmeal, almonds and sugar in a large bowl. Using fingertips, rub in butter until mixture resembles coarse breadcrumbs. Stir in vegetable oil, then add combined eggs, vanilla and lemon rind and stir until well combined. Pour batter into a well-greased, base-lined 26cm springform pan, smooth top and bake at 180C for 35-40 minutes or until top is golden and a cake tester withdraws clean. Stand in pan for 10 minutes, then turn out on a wire rack to cool. Serve dusted with icing sugar. Cake will keep in an airtight container for up to 1 week.

**Serves 12-14**

# Caramelised pineapple and citrus fruits with spiced muscat cream

300g (1⅓ cups) caster sugar

Thinly peeled strip of lemon rind

1 star anise

2 cloves

1 vanilla bean, split lengthways

1 small pineapple (about 800g)

2 oranges

2 ruby oranges or blood oranges

1 teaspoon olive oil

250g mascarpone

1 tablespoon muscat

Combine 220g (1 cup) sugar, lemon rind, spices, scraped seeds from vanilla bean and bean with ½ cup water in a small saucepan and stir over medium heat until sugar dissolves. Remove from heat and cool. Remove ¼ cup of syrup and reserve for spiced muscat cream.

Peel pineapple, cut small grooves in a spiral to remove "eyes" from pineapple, then cut into 1cm-thick slices. Remove rind and pith from oranges and cut into 1cm-thick slices.

Sprinkle slices of fruit with remaining sugar. Brush a non-stick frying pan with olive oil and heat, then cook slices of fruit, in batches, until lightly caramelised. Transfer to a flat dish, pour over cooled syrup mixture and cool to room temperature or refrigerate until needed.

Place mascarpone and muscat in a bowl and stir until combined, then, using a wooden spoon, gradually stir in reserved syrup until mixture is well combined and the consistency of thick cream. Serve caramelised pineapple and citrus fruits with spiced muscat cream.

Serves 6

# Baked lemon polenta puddings with currant syrup

100g (½ cup, firmly packed) light brown sugar

2 egg yolks

200g (1 cup) ricotta

2 teaspoons grated lemon rind

¼ cup lemon juice

80g butter, melted

50g polenta

2 tablespoons self-raising flour

4 egg whites

Syrup

75g (⅓ cup) caster sugar

25g currants

1 tablespoon lemon juice

For syrup, combine all ingredients and ¼ cup water in a saucepan, stir over medium heat until sugar dissolves, bring to the boil, then set aside.

Using an electric mixer, beat sugar and egg yolks until very thick and pale. Add ricotta and lemon rind and beat until smooth, then add lemon juice and beat until well combined. Using a wooden spoon, stir in butter, polenta and flour and mix well.

Using an electric mixer, beat egg whites until firm peaks form, then fold into polenta mixture, in two batches, until just combined. Divide pudding mixture among 6 greased 100-125ml small cups or ramekins, place on an oven tray and bake at 180C for 25 minutes or until lightly browned and puffed. Remove from oven and stand for 5 minutes (puddings will deflate slightly) before brushing with a little of the hot syrup and sprinkling with currants. Serve puddings warm with remaining syrup passed separately.

**Serves 6**

# Pan-fried pears with honey and walnuts

60g butter, chopped
4 beurre bosc pears, cut into 5mm-thick slices
¼ cup honey
1 teaspoon finely grated orange rind
2 tablespoons Grand Marnier or other orange-flavoured liqueur
40g walnuts, roasted and chopped
Double cream, to serve

Melt 40g butter in a large frying pan, add half the pear slices and cook for 2 minutes on each side or until golden. Remove pears with a slotted spoon and cook remaining pears, then remove from pan. Add remaining butter, honey, orange rind, liqueur and walnuts to pan and, stirring continuously, bring to the boil, then remove from heat. Divide pears among bowls or plates, drizzle with a little sauce and serve with a spoonful of double cream.

Serves 4

ACIDULATED WATER: water with lemon juice added, to prevent discolouration of vegetables and fruits once peeled.

AGED BALSAMIC VINEGAR: a fragrant, sweetish vinegar from Modena, Italy, made from concentrated grape juice and aged in wooden barrels for at least 10 years.

BAKING POWDER: a raising agent that is two parts cream of tartar to one part bicarbonate of soda (baking soda).

BEETROOT: beets or red beets.

BLACK MUSTARD SEEDS: a strong, pungent variety of mustard seed used in curries.

BUTTER: use salted or unsalted (sweet) butter as directed (125g is equal to one stick of butter).

CANNELLINI BEANS: small dried white beans (also available in cans).

CAPSICUM: also known as pepper or bell pepper. Discard seeds and membranes.

CASTER SUGAR: superfine or finely granulated table sugar.

CHAT POTATO: baby new potato.

CORIANDER: also known as cilantro or chinese parsley.

CORNICHON: tiny sour French gherkin.

CORNMEAL: see polenta.

CREME FRAICHE: cultured thick cream, with a fresh, sour taste. Does not separate when boiled.

CRISP FRIED SHALLOTS: usually served as a condiment or sprinkled over food. Available from Asian food stores.

DASHI: the basic fish and seaweed stock that provides the distinctive flavour of many Japanese dishes. Made from dried bonito flakes and kelp (kombu), it is available from Asian food stores. Instant dashi powder, also known as dashi-no-moto, is a concentrated granular form.

EGGPLANT: aubergine.

FLAGEOLET BEANS: type of haricot bean with a delicate flavour, that ranges in colour from pale green to creamy white. Used in French cooking.

FLORAL HONEY: the best style of honey for cakes, syrups and desserts. Varieties include orange blossom, salvation jane, clover.

FONTINA: a semi-hard Northern Italian cheese with a nutty flavour similar to gruyère.

FRENCH-TRIMMED: bone ends cleaned of meat.

FROZEN SHELLED SOY BEANS: available from Asian food stores.

GARAM MASALA: a roasted, ground blend of spices originating in North India, based on cardamom, cinnamon, cloves, coriander, fennel and cumin.

GREEN ONION: sometimes called shallot or scallion, an immature onion pulled when the top is still green and before the bulb has formed. Sold by the bunch.

HARISSA: fiery paste from North Africa, usually made from fresh or dried red chillies, garlic, olive oil and caraway seeds. Available from some supermarkets, delicatessens and Middle Eastern food stores.

JULIENNE: vegetables, fruit or citrus rinds cut approximately 3mm thick in 25mm strips.

KECAP MANIS: Indonesian sweet soy sauce. Available from Asian food stores and supermarkets.

MIRIN: sweet rice wine, used only in cooking. Found in Asian food stores; substitute sweet sherry.

MUSCAT: Liqueur muscat is an aged sweet fortified wine.

MUSHROOM
*Shiitake*: also known as chinese black, forest or golden oak; large and meaty with an earthy taste. *Shimeji*: mild-flavoured, firm-textured variety resembling small oyster mushrooms. *Swiss brown*: full-bodied flavour, also known as roman or cremini. Substitute button or cap variety.

MUSHROOM OYSTER SAUCE: vegetarian oyster sauce.

ORANGE FLOWER WATER: a perfumed flavouring made from distilled orange blossoms.

ORZO: tiny rice-shaped pasta.

OUZO: aniseed-flavoured liqueur.

PALM SUGAR: also known as nam tan pip, jaggery, jawa or gula melaka; made from the sap of the sugar palm tree. Sold in a variety of forms, from soft to very hard.

PECORINO: a dry, sharp, salty sheep's milk cheese.

PIN-BONE: to remove small bones from fish, using tweezers.

POLENTA: yellow-white coarse granular meal made from maize or corn. Also known as cornmeal.

POMEGRANATE MOLASSES: made from the juice of pomegranate seeds boiled down to a thick syrup. Available from delicatessens and Middle Eastern food stores.

PRESERVED LEMON: lemons preserved in salt and lemon juice. A North African specialty.

PUY LENTILS: very fine, dark blue-green lentils originally from Le Puy, France. Available from good delicatessens.

RAS EL HANOUT: ground spice mix from North Africa. Available from spice stores and Middle Eastern food stores.

ROSEWATER: aromatic extract made from crushed rose petals, known as gulab in India.

SAFFRON THREADS: threads from the dried stigmas of the crocus flower. Found in good food stores and some supermarkets.

SAMBAL OELEK: Indonesian chilli paste made from pounded chillies, salt, vinegar or tamarind.

SHALLOTS: also known as eschalots or french shallots. Small golden brown bulbs, grown in clusters and sold by weight.

SICHUAN PEPPER (szechuan pepper): a mildly hot spice with a distinctive flavour and fragrance made from the dried berry of the prickly ash tree. Available from Asian food stores in whole or powdered form.

SPANISH ONION: a purplish-red onion with a mild flavour. Also known as red onion.

TAMARIND PASTE: made from the soft dried pulp of the tamarind pod. Thick and purplish black, available from Asian food stores.

VERJUICE: unfermented grape juice, with a delicate lemon-vinegar flavour. Available from delicatessens.

VINE LEAVES IN BRINE: can be salty so rinse before use; available from delicatessens and some supermarkets.

WASHED-RIND CHEESE: first surface-ripened by bacteria, then washed, it has an orange or white rind and a strong smell.

ZUCCHINI: courgette.

# measures

One Australian metric measuring cup holds approximately 250ml, one Australian metric tablespoon holds 20ml, one Australian metric teaspoon holds 5ml. The difference between one country's measuring cups and another's is within a two- or three-teaspoon variance. North America, New Zealand and the United Kingdom use a 15ml tablespoon.

All cup and spoon measurements are level.

We use large eggs with an average weight of 60g.

Unless specified, all fruit and vegetables are medium sized and herbs are fresh.

## DRY MEASURES

| metric | imperial |
|---|---|
| 15g | ½oz |
| 30g | 1oz |
| 60g | 2oz |
| 90g | 3oz |
| 125g | 4oz (¼lb) |
| 155g | 5oz |
| 185g | 6oz |
| 220g | 7oz |
| 250g | 8oz (½lb) |
| 280g | 9oz |
| 315g | 10oz |
| 345g | 11oz |
| 375g | 12oz (¾lb) |
| 410g | 13oz |
| 440g | 14oz |
| 470g | 15oz |
| 500g | 16oz (1lb) |
| 750g | 24oz (1½lb) |
| 1kg | 32oz (2lb) |

## LIQUID MEASURES

| metric | imperial |
|---|---|
| 30ml | 1 fluid oz |
| 60ml | 2 fluid oz |
| 100ml | 3 fluid oz |
| 125ml | 4 fluid oz |
| 150ml | 5 fluid oz (¼ pint/1 gill) |
| 190ml | 6 fluid oz |
| 250ml | 8 fluid oz |
| 300ml | 10 fluid oz (½ pint) |
| 500ml | 16 fluid oz |
| 600ml | 20 fluid oz (1 pint) |
| 1000ml (1 litre) | 1¾ pints |

## LENGTH MEASURES

| metric | imperial |
|---|---|
| 3mm | ⅛in |
| 6mm | ¼in |
| 1cm | ½in |
| 2cm | ¾in |
| 2.5cm | 1in |
| 5cm | 2in |
| 6cm | 2½in |
| 8cm | 3in |
| 10cm | 4in |
| 13cm | 5in |
| 15cm | 6in |
| 18cm | 7in |
| 20cm | 8in |
| 23cm | 9in |
| 25cm | 10in |
| 28cm | 11in |
| 30cm | 12in (1ft) |

## OVEN TEMPERATURES

These oven temperatures are only a guide. Always check the manufacturer's manual.

| | °C (Celsius) | °F (Fahrenheit) | Gas Mark |
|---|---|---|---|
| Very slow | 120 | 250 | 1 |
| Slow | 150 | 300 | 2 |
| Moderately slow | 160 | 325 | 3 |
| Moderate | 180-190 | 350-375 | 4 |
| Moderately hot | 200-210 | 400-425 | 5 |
| Hot | 220-230 | 450-475 | 6 |
| Very hot | 240-250 | 500-525 | 7 |